ROY CHUBBY BROWN

UNZIPPED

ROY CHUBBY BROWN

UNZIPPED

with
MARK LEIGH
and
MIKE LEPINE

B🌳XTREE

First published in Great Britain in 1995 by Boxtree Limited,
Broadwall House, 21 Broadwall, London SE1 9PL
Copyright © Roy "Chubby" Brown 1995
10 9 8 7 6 5 4 3 2 1
ISBN: 0 7522 0761 X

A CIP catalogue entry for this book is available from the British Library.
Design by Design 23.
Printed and bound in the United Kingdom by Cambus Litho Ltd, East Kilbride.

PICTURE CREDITS

Page 15: © Mike Hewitt/Marc Morrison/Gray Mortimore/Allsport
Pages 28–29: © Brendan O'Sullivan/John C. Jacques/Retna
Pages 58–59: © Michael Putland/Retna

DEDICATION

This book is dedicated to that rare group of men who have been blessed by mother nature with the rare ability to gobble themselves.
Roy 'Chubby' Brown

P.S. Many thanks to all my fans who sent me get-well cards and messages of sympathy after my recent back injury.
P.P.S. This book is not – I repeat NOT – dedicated to Middlesbrough town council who refuse to let me perform in my home town. They can just piss off.

PUBLISHER'S APOLOGY

We're really, really sorry about this book.

COMPLAINING ABOUT THIS BOOK

The publishers and authors are happy to receive all complaints about this book. Please type your comments double spaced on A4 paper, quoting reference CB/64/8/d on each sheet submitted. Please fold your letter to A5 and attach a stamped addressed envelope. Then shove the whole lot up your arse.

ERRATUM

Please note the following printer's errors in this book:
Page 23: In the feature about Princess Diana the word 'nob' should be replaced by the words 'ice cream'
Page 47: In the feature about Noel Edmonds, the word 'mental' should be replaced by the phrase 'happy go lucky'
Page 71: In the biography of Anthea Turner, the phrase 'like a train' should be replaced by the phrase 'to bed early because of her demanding TV schedule'
Page 87: The phrase 'played hide the cucumber' should be replaced by the phrase 'declared Parliament open'.
Page 94: In the feature on Hugh Grant, the word 'handsome' should be replaced by the word 'arsehole'

CONTENTS

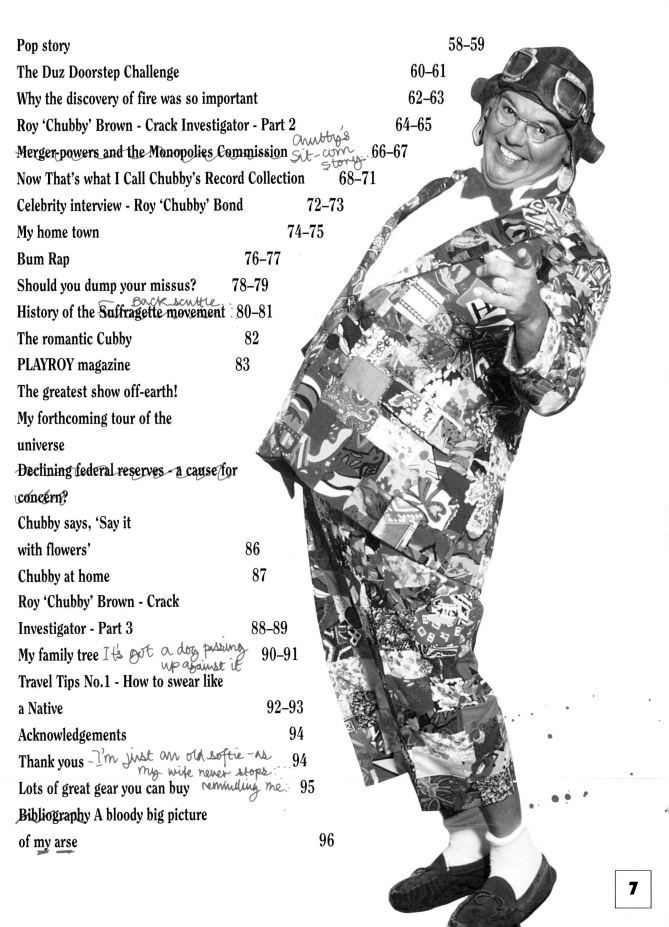

MY CLOSE FRIENDSHIP WITH PAUL SIMON

Back in the early 1960s, at one club I found myself sharing the bill with a very young and then unknown Paul Simon. I'll never forget sitting on a railway platform with him late one night after a show. I started singing, and he started strumming along on guitar. Magic. You know, it could so easily have been Simon and Chubby....If I remember rightly, our song went something like this..

> *We're sitting in a railway station*
> *Indulging in some masturbation*
> *Yeah, mmm-mmm!*
> *Out of luck on one night stands*
> *So it's trousers down and nobs in hands*
> *All pumping flesh and swollen glans*
> *It's nice to have a good hand-shand...*

Later on, the short-arsed bastard just changed the lyrics and made a fortune! Come on Paul - release the original! (And don't think I've forgotten what 'Slip Sliding Away' is really about, either...)

WONDERS OF THE NORTHERN WORLD No1.
CHUBBY'S SWEAR BOX

HOW TO EXPLAIN THE
FACTS OF LIFE TO YOUR CHILD

THE CHUBBY CURRENCY

People often come up to me after a show and say "Chubby, you're a man of the world. What do you think of a common European currency?".

Well I say bollocks to the European Exchange Mechanism and all that shite. Mind you, I think we should change our currency – pounds and pence are so bloody boring.

The Americans nearly got it right when they called their currency 'cents'...think about it. Even the French had a better idea, making sure that 'Francs' rhymes with 'wanks'. Clever buggers!

What I think we need is a currency with names to make it more interesting. This is what I suggest:-

100 Nobs = 1 Chuff
10 Pussies = 20 Nobs
25 Willies = 1 Pussy
5 Bums = 10 Willies
1 Bollock = 2 Bums

This way it would be a lot more interesting.
These are some of the conversations you'd be having:

Two Bollocks

A Nob

Hey Chubby. Can you lend me a Bum 'til I'm straight.

Excuse me, have you got a Pussy for two Nobs?

I've just put a Willie in this slot but nothing came out.

This Nob must be brand new. It's all shiney.

I've just been to the bank. I've got a wad of Chuff in my wallet.

I'm so skint I haven't got two Bollocks to rub together!

Let's toss a Willie to see who goes first.

My grandmother showed me her Royal Jubilee commemorative Pussy.

THE Chubby CHANNEL

CHUBBY CHOICE

Now available on satellite and cable! Guaranteed! 24 hour filth and depravity. No culture here, mate! (The only culture I know is the one growing between my wife's legs that's got all the gynaecologists baffled).

5.00 OPEN ALL HOURS
Return of the popular sit-com about my wife's twat. Broadcast in Widescreen.

5.30 AUF WEIDERSEIN PET
Bittersweet hard-core German sex comedy about a pervert forced to leave the one true love of his life - his alsatian.

6.30 PRO-CELEBRITY FROTTAGE
Sad sexual inadequates join top celebrities to rub themselves up against objects and unsuspecting members of the public.

7.00 GET IT UP
New quiz show! My missus strips naked and our guest celebrity team have just 45 minutes to try and get an erection. Play along at home with Chubby's £1 million 'Don't fancy yours mate' challenge!

7.45 THE NEW ADVENTURERS OF HAMMY HAMSTER
This week's star guest is Richard Gere. Last in series.

7.46 RUDE CLASSICS
Boring old classics made absolutely 100% stonking filthy!
This week *The Nobhound of the Baskervilles*.
Future classics in this series include:
Tightarse Andronicus, Great Ejaculations, A Midsummer's Night Wet Dream, Fanny by Gaslight, A Tale of Two Titties, Wuthering Shites, Toss of the D'Urbevilles, Northwhanger Abbey, Moby Dyke, Treasure Arsehole and *David Copafeel*.

UNZIPPED

EXCLUSIVE TO THE CHUBBY CHANNEL

ALL THE TOP SPORTING ACTION FROM THE 'SWEARING OLYMPICS'!

SECOND ROUND MEN'S RELAY

BOXING QUARTER FINALS
- a real test of stamina and vocabulary!

MARATHON The Swearing Marathon 50 yards from the finish line this contestant was disqualified on the grounds that 'jam puff' is not a recognised swearword under IOC rules.

15

12.00 THE EUROVISION DONG CONTEST
Thrilling battle between members of the European Union.

1.00 HOW DO THEY DO THAT?
Is Penis enlargement possible? This is part 1 of an 84 part series in which I search the world looking for an answer.

1.30 WHY DO THEY DO THAT?
Tonight's subjects include felching, fisting and sleeping with Fatima Whitbread.

2.00 BLIND SHAG!
I get to shag three contestants and, based on that, decide which one I actually want to speak to afterwards.

3.25 STRIP MASTERMIND
This week Melvyn Bragg and Stephen Hawkin take on Linda Lusardi and that bird in the ad who says she 'moves with the times' – so it should be OK to watch!

3.30 THE WEE-WEE HOURS
Special late-night programme for 'shower' enthusiasts. See the best from 'The Golden Shot' and 'The Golden Girls', plus music from Wet Wet Wet.

4.30 PILLOW TALK
Annabel Giles, Elizabeth Hurley and Anthea Turner talk about their most intimate desires, while I go off behind a screen.

6.00 DON'T FORGET YOUR DIAPHRAGM
The lucky contestant wins a once in a lifetime trip to Chubby's bedroom (this might not sound like much but it's better than being humiliated on live TV by some ginger prat).

7.00 THE BLOODY GOOD LIFE
Happy-go-lucky comedian Roy 'Chubby' Brown shares a flat with two nymphomaniacs who have a never-explained bathtub full of semolina.

7.30 THE SOUTH WANK SHOW
Previewing new XXXX films coming your way on the Chubby Channel, including *When Bimbos Undress, Mega-Jugs III and IV, Shaven Frenzy, Whipmaidens of Planet Shagg, Bold n' Bosomy, Hot n' Horny, Big n' Bouncy, Firm n' Fruity, Damp n' Dirty, Blondes n' Bondage, Rough n' Ready* and *Pube Divers II – Beyond the Vulva.*

8.30 MUFFIN THE MULE
Not for the normal.

9.00 SNATCH OF THE DAY
Blow-by-blow account including all the best shots and plenty of action in the box. Exclusive interview with Gazza who complains bitterly that his manager always pulls him off at half time.

10.00 ANIMAL ACTION!
XXXXXXXX rated pervie movie festival.
See panel for details.

ANIMALS ARE IN SEASON AGAIN ON THE CHUBBY CHANNEL!

Just look at some of the great XXXX animal action films coming your way over the next month...

- Hog Tied!
- Porkie Gets Porked
- House Trained And Horny!
- Bonking Badgers (Widescreen)
- Ride 'em Cowboy
- Invertebrate Orgy
- And Dobbin Made Three
- Cock-A-Doodle Do
- Big Udders II (Uncut)
- Barnyard Discipline
- Goosie, Goosie, Gander!
- Bare Back Rodeo
- Spread Eagled!
- Squeek Piggy, Squeek! (Stereo)
- Doggie Position
- Emmanuelle Meets The Wombats

- Hen House Rendezvous
- Kennel Club (Directors Cut)
- Horse Play
- Passion for Pizzle
- Led Astray
- How The Kittens Lost Their Mittens
- Hamster Romance!
- Debbie Does Battersea
- Finned Floozies (XXX!)
- Out To Stud
- Bedtime For Bonzo
- Cock-a-too!
- Horny From Hibernating
- Horny Toad! (Edited for language)
- The Educating Of Joey
- The Devil In Fido

As Britain's bluest comedian, I think I've got a duty to forge ahead and introduce the next generation of obscenities. Don't thank me, just start using them right away...

BROWN'S RUDER OXFORD DICK TIONARY

CHUBBY PRESS

AGASSI [n] Noxious discharge. Typical use; *I'm not going down on you, I can smell the* Agassi *from here!*

BROWN [n] A really, really huge massive enormous penis that you'd be proud to have in your trousers. Typical use; *Feast your eyes on this* Brown, *girls!*

CLINTON [n] A pubic crab. Typical use; *I can't stop scratching – me pubes are crawling with* Clintons!

FERGIE [n] A semi-erect nob that's no use to anyone.

GAZZA [n] A quick shag on the floor of a public toilet.

GROLSCH [v] To Grolsch. To accidentally sit on your partner's testicles during intercourse.

HESELTINE [n] That strange fluid that leaks out of your Japseye before you come off proper.

HURD [n] Erection. Typical use *I've got a* Hurd-*on the size of an elephant.*

KINNOCK [n] A Japseye.

LEMMY [n] A Skidmark. Typical use; *Just look at these* Lemmies! *You can wash your own underpants!*

MINOGUE [n] Crusted-on nob cheese.

MULLER [v] To vomit. Typical use; Mulllllllllerrrrrrrr!

NOAKES [n] Collective word for sores on your willy. Typical use; *Don't come near me with that! It's covered in* Noakes!

ORANJEBOOM [v] To Oranjeboom. To backscuttle.

PORTILLO [n] An arsehole. Typical use; *Come on Sailor boy, pack my* Portillo! *You're talking out of your* Portillo!

RIFKIND [v or n] To Rifkind. The act of masturbation. Typical uses; *Oy,* Rifkind! or *I'm going to have one off the* Rifkind.

TEBBIT [n] A small, shrivelly, wrinkled and unsightly penis.

WALDEGRAVE [n] A particularly big and prominant tit.

CHUBBY ON THE BOX

I may be a top comedy star, but my appearances on TV have been very few and far between. And none of the bastards have ever, ever been broadcast.

I didn't have much luck with Jackanory, but I still think The Story of O is very educational....

And my career with Blue Peter didn't get beyond demonstrating a very novel use for an old Squeezie bottle...

I was so desperate to get on Telly, I even appeared on an interview programme with Sue Lawley

I keep sending ideas in, and volunteering for shows, but I never seem to get nowhere...

Dear Mr Brown,

Thank you for your interest in London Weekend Television programming and your recent suggestions.
In response to the points you raise
A] Network centre would certainly veto any programme called 'Celebrity Cunnilingus', whether or not the programme was 'tastefully done' [is that your idea of a joke?]
B] Ditto 'Swallow this!'
C] Matthew Kelly is very proud of the work he does on YOU BET and would never allow a bet on whether or not you could have sex with 30 cheerleaders in two minutes.
D] BLIND DATE is not rigged. We therefore cannot guarantee to fix you up with 'some big breasted Essex tart' in exchange for some 'red hot footage that'll double the ratings'. I also regret that we cannot give you the home telephone number of 'the dim one who looks like she goes like a bloody train', not least because that vague description covers most of our contestants.
E] No, you cannot appear on SURPRISE! SURPRISE! and you can certainly not do that to Cilla.
F] You are not alone in writing in to request that we do this to Michael Barrymore. However, he still has several years on his contract and to perform he needs to be able to walk.
G] Regardless of what you have in your underpants, Michael Aspel will not come round to look at it for STRANGE BUT TRUE?
H] While we are proud of our record of catering for minority interests, a programme featuring just sheep in exotic leather apparel would be far too specialist to gain an audience.
I] BAYWATCH is made in America. We have no say as to whether the women keep their swimsuits on or not.
J] We are always looking for a new format for chat shows, but one that mixes 'celebrity gossip with golden showers' will never be broadcast.
K] I have never asked Cilla if she does, and so I am afraid it will be impossible to send you some.

NETWORK CENTRE
ITV HOUSE

Dear Mr Brown,

As I have said before, in at least twenty previous letters, we cannot offer you a spot on ITV for 'The Roy Chubby Brown Show'. You are *not* a family entertainer, despite your claim to have personally entertained three members of my immediate family. I am also returning your unsolicited script for your proposed sit-com 'WELL BUGGER ME' - about which less said, the better, quite frankly...

WELL BUGGER ME!

EPISODE 1;   THE BOSS COMES TO VISIT

CHARACTERS:
ROY – A CHARMING, CHEEKY WORKING MAN
DORIS – HIS WIFE

SET:LIVING ROOM –   TERRACED HOUSE IN MIDDLESBROUGH

ROY; I'm home. Get me a bloody drink would you love?
I'm as dry as a pensioner's twat!

DORIS; [FROM KITCHEN] Sodding get it yourself. I've got
my hands busy at the moment

ROY; Aw, you could have done that before I got home!
[TO CAMERA] Bloody fish fingers again tonight!

DORIS; [FROM KITCHEN] I'm cooking. Have you forgot your
boss is coming over our house?

ROY; [TO CAMERA] It'll make a change from coming over
his secretary.

DORIS; [FROM KITCHEN] I've got the house all nice, so
don't stink it out with your farts, Roy!

ROY; Cheeky cow! [TO CAMERA] They put her fanny farts
on the weather forecast. Sodding gales in Middlesbrough.

DORIS; [FROM KITCHEN] You leave my fanny alone!

ROY; [STICKS HEAD AROUND KITCHEN DOOR] Why? Are you
trying to be faithful to the milkman again?

DORIS; Leave me alone! I've got a load on my plate...

ROY; What, the milkman missed your tits again, did he?

CHUBBY CHAT!

REAL LIFE XXXXX SEX LINES - THE MOST REALISTIC ADULT PHONE SEX LINES IN THE WORLD!!!!!!!!!!

BUSTY 18 YEAR OLD TURNS YOU DOWN FLAT!   0898-4321

RANDY LESBIANS DON'T WANT YOU ANYWHERE NEAR THEM!   0898-4721

BORED MIDDLE AGED HOUSEWIFE HAS HEADACHE!   0898-4381

SEXY BLONDE VIXEN LAUGHS AT SMALL COCKS!   0898-4341

DD STUDENT WOULDN'T GIVE YOU A SECOND LOOK!   0898-4331

RANDY MANDY, NIGHT NURSE, TELLS YOU TO 'PISS OFF LOSER!'   0898-4311

18 YEAR OLD NYMPHETTE WANTS YOU TO BUY HER DRINKS AND THEN SHOVE OFF!   0898-4391

NAUGHTY NICOLE DOESN'T DO IT WITH PRATS!   0898-4323

DD BLAMMERS – PUT YOUR FACE IN BETWEEN THEM AND GET HAULED UP ON CHARGES!   0898-4324

INSATIABLE NYMPHO HAS CRABS!   0898-4325

I'LL SNUB YOU!   0898-4326

DRUNK AND HORNY TWO-TIMING HOUSEWIFE WILL FLIRT WITH YOU, THROW UP DOWN YOUR SHIRT AND PASS OUT!   0898-432

GORGEOUS REDHEAD FANCIES YOUR BEST MATE!   0898-4328

MY PANTIES ARE DRIPPING - I HAVE A WEAK BLADDER. SORRY.   0898-4329

I'M HOT AND HORNY - BUT NOT FOR YOU!   0898-1321

CHASTISE ME - I'VE OVERSPENT ON YOUR CREDIT CARD AGAIN! 0898-2321

JUICY LUCY IS WAITING FOR YOU – TO GET IT UP!   0898-3321

HORNY SEX- BOMB MAKES YOU COME TOO SOON!   0898-3321

RING THIS NUMBER FROM WORK EVERY DAY AND GET THE SACK   0898-3523

I'VE BEEN A NAUGHTY GIRL – I'VE BROKEN INTO YOUR CAR AND STOLEN YOUR RADIO!   0898-6321

DDD CURVY BLONDE LOVE SLUT SCARES THE SHIT OUT OF YOU!

0898-7321

LUSCIOUS LISA THINKS YOU'RE CREEPY! 0898-8321

DIRTY DONNA DOES IT WITH ANYONE – WHAT A PITY YOU'LL NEVER MEET HER! 0898-9321

I'M NOT WEARING PANTIES OR KNICKERS – I'M SENILE! 0898-0321

MY NIPPLES ARE SWOLLEN – I'M LACTATING! 0898-4331

WANK YOURSELF OFF WHILE YOU WASTE LOTS OF MONEY 0898-4323

All calls charged at 36p per minute off peak and 48p per minute at all other times.

HOUSEWIVES' HOTLINE– YOUR INNERMOST FANTASIES – *FULFILLED!*

THE DAY I WON NEW SOFA COVERS!
0898-4361

LOCKED IN SAINSBURY'S   0898-4326

FREEMANS SENT ME A DRESS BY MISTAKE! 0898- 4321

QUEEN OF MY LOCAL WEIGHTWATCHERS 0898-4421

CHEAP JAFFAS AT KWIK-SAVE
0898-4341

BARGAIN BIN GRAB FRENZY
0898-4324

LAST PARKING SPACE AT ASDA
0898-4521

52 WEEKS AT 38p/WEEK!   0898-4387

SHE NEVER CHARGED ME FOR THE CUP- A- SOUPS! 0898-4621

FULL SHOLLEY 0898- 4721

NEW HAT! 0898- 8321

LO-CAL CHOCOLATE ECLAIR BREAKTHROUGH! 0898-4921

0% FINANCE! 0898-4421

All calls charged at 36p per minute off peak and 48p per minute at all other times.

U
N
Z
I
P
P
E
D

CHUBBY'S TIPS FOR A HAPPIER SEX LIFE No.1

HOW TO GIVE A GIRL AN ORGASM

CHUBBY'S TIPS FOR A HAPPIER SEX LIFE – No.2

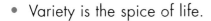

GET A BIT ON THE SIDE: WHY YOU SHOULD CHEAT ON YOUR WIFE

- Variety is the spice of life.
- It gives her a rest.
- Her sister is younger than she is.
- There's nothing on telly.
- Quiche and salad is not a proper dinner for a working man.
- She shouldn't be having a period.
- She shouldn't be having a baby.
- Kings Cross is holding a '2 for the price of 1' sale.
- Your wife doesn't own a figure-hugging red waspie.
  (and if she did she'd look pretty sad in it.)
- She's the wrong side of 40.
- Why break the habit of a lifetime?
- You were brought up to share what you have.
- Desiree is a nice name.
- It gives her more free time to clean the house and do the shopping.
- Who knows when you'll get the opportunity again?
- It would be nice to make love to someone of the 'opposite sex' again.
- It would be nice to touch the sides for once.
- It's a very French thing to do and we're supposed to be Europeans these days…
- You've been married more than six months.
- There's no law against it.
- Because you can.

YOUR BIT ON THE SIDE SAYS...

Give me your length

I want you

Paint my belly!

Make me come

I'm going to blow your mind

I've got the hots for you

You're so big!

Take me to heaven and back!

You make me feel like a woman

THE WIFE SAYS–

Give me your pay packet

I want you to stop wearing those awful
socks for weeks at a time

Paint the skirting board!

Make me a new kitchen cupboard

I'm going to blow your life savings

I've got a headache

You're so big. I'm putting you on a
diet, you fat pig

Take me round my mother's house

You make me feel sick to my stomach

I love S & M	I love M & S
Let's go to bed	Let's go to Tescos
Strip me!	Strip the walls in the spare room!
Eat me!	Eat it - it's all you're getting!
I need you inside me	I need a new coat
Leave it in...	Leave it out...
I'm coming	I'm going
How do you like this new basque and suspenders set?	How do you like this new saucepan?
It's so hard	It's so hard living with you
You're all man	You're all talk
I've got the hots!	I've got cystitis
I've never felt so full	Is it in?
Let's do it again!	zzzzzzzzzzzzzzzzz!

CHUBBY GOES TO HOLLYWOOD

After the success of my mega-platinum-multi-Oscar-winning film UFO, I have been inundated with offers to work in Hollywood. The film has made me an international star. I know you loved it, because everywhere I go, people yell 'UFO!' at me.   Here are just some of the exciting projects I'm involved with at the moment..

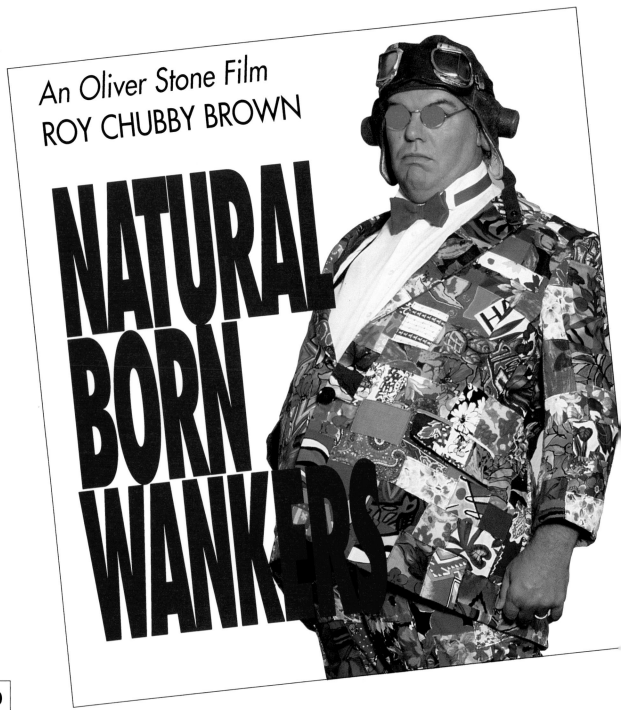

An Oliver Stone Film
ROY CHUBBY BROWN

NATURAL BORN WANKERS

THE FLY

BE AFRAID. BE VERY AFRAID.

Hello Dolly!

FROM THE MAKERS OF **GUYS AND DOLLS**

They're even talking about putting me in a special new 'Director's Cut' of 'Reservoir Dogs'...

Five Total Strangers
Team Up For The Perfect Crime.
They Don't Know Each Other's Name.
But They've Got Each Other's Number.

RESERVOIR DOGS

HARVEY KEITEL TIM ROTH CHRIS PENN STEVE BUSCEMI LAWRENCE TIERNEY AND MICHAEL MADSEN

These are my test shots for the forthcoming blockbuster,

WHEN CHUBBY MET SALLY.

Ohhhh! Squeal! Gasp! Yes! Yes! Yes! Oh God, yes, yes, yes, yes! No! No! yes! Yes! Ahhhhhhhh

WOMAN; I'll have what she's having
CHUBBY; OK love - just let me wipe me fucking fingers clean first...

ROY CHUBBY BROWN IN

SHAG FRENZY!

CO-STARRING

MICHELLE PFEIFFER

as 'BJ'

But, if it were up to me, these are the films I'd really like to star in...

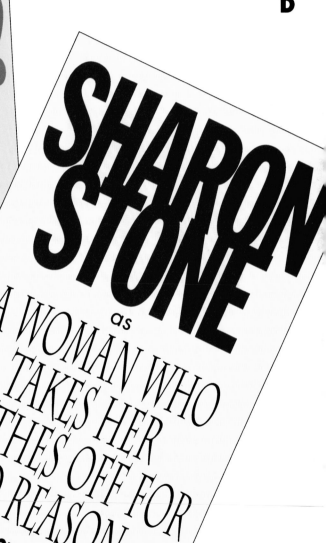

SHARON STONE

as

A WOMAN WHO TAKES HER CLOTHES OFF FOR NO REASON WITH ROY CHUBBY BROWN

CHUBBY BROWN

Wank away Weight with
MR. MASTURBATOR

MEN – KEEP SLIM AND TRIM BY HAVING ONE OFF THE WRIST!

Yo readers! If you bought my last exercise video
SHAPE UP AND SHAG
you'll know that each time you screw you burn up
150 calories. Well I've been investigating wanking as a way
to weight loss and I was sodding amazed, I was.

Each time you have a J Arthur you burn up 85 calories!
What's more, you can keep flabby wrists trim and
supple into the bargain!

In this new video I demonstrate 21 different wanking
workouts – each one to a different hit song.
Wank along with me and follow the simple moves from the
basic 'five finger shuffle' to the more advanced 'rolling the
dough' or 'spanking the monkey' and you'll see the pounds
dropping off in front of your eyes
(unless your bloody eyesight goes first, that is).

And you don't need to join any fancy gym or health club.
You can wank away weight in the comfort and privacy
of your own home
(providing it's got curtains and the wife's out).

Just look at the sensational soundtrack:

- Pull your plonker to 'Only The Lonely' by Roy Orbison
- Flong your dong to 'You Need Hands' by Max Bygraves
- Beat your meat to 'Don't Stop 'Til You Get Enough' by Michael Jackson
- Jack off to 'I Just Don't Know What To Do With Myself' by Dusty Springfield
- Bang the bishop to 'Lonely Boy' by Andrew Gold
- Flog your log to 'Are You Lonesome Tonight' by Elvis Presley
- Go jerkin' your gherkin to 'Careless Hands' by Des O'Connor
- Slam your spam to 'Enjoy Yourself' by The Jacksons
- Twitch your tadger to 'Hey Girl Don't Bother Me' by The Tams
- Shoot the tadpoles to 'Slowhand' by Eric Clapton
- Toss yourself off to 'The Greatest Love Of All' by Whitney Houston
- Kneed your knob to 'Under My Thumb' by the Rolling Stones
- Stretch your sausage to 'Whole Lotta Shakin' Goin' On' by Little Richard
- Tug your todger to 'All By Myself' by Eric Carmen
- Pack your palm to 'Does You Mother Know' by Abba
- Rub your rhythm stick to 'It Only Takes A Minute' by Tavares
- Stroke your salami to 'No Woman No Cry' by Bob Marley
- Pump your pecker to 'Me, Myself I' by Joan Armatrading
- Have a hand shandy to 'I Can't Help Myself' by The Four Tops
- Turn Japanese to 'I'm Turning Japanese' by the Vapours

Especially recommended for solicitors, estate agents, my home town councillors, Dixons shop assistants.

WATCH OUT FOR MY OTHER EXERCISE VIDEOS IN THE SHOPS
- Lose 2lbs a day the Back Scuttle Way • The Gobble-Gobble Protein Diet
- The Sit On My Face And Wriggle Health Plan
- Shit yourself lighter – the Vindaloo Workout
- Work your Helmet! – the 21 day Glans Plan

MINGLING WITH THE MIGHTY

I love knocking around with the Royals! I'm still a simple Geordie lad at heart, but the posh nobs love my act every bit as much as everyone else – and they're all clamouring to meet me.

The Royals, in particular, are my greatest fans. Princess Margaret runs my fan club and Phil's always saying, 'have you heard this one, Chubbs?' and then telling me a filthy joke I couldn't even do in my act! No wonder they say they're blue blooded!

Whenever I've got a spare moment, I'll pop down the Palace to see them. It has to be a secret though, and they insist I come up the tradesman's entrance. That is, unless Prince Edward's using it.

I envy Phil. I mean, his wife's the queen. He *knows* she's not knocking off the milkman, right? They probably don't even have a milkman they're so posh. And you know because she's royalty that she keeps her legs shaved, for all those walkabouts she does. Unlike my missus who has to give her legs a shampoo and set every week.

And he knows that when he's out trooping the colour or doing some other bollocks his missus isn't going through his wallet for bingo money because she's the Queen and she's got more bastard money than she knows what to do with.

I'm not surprised that, on the two or three occasions I've suggested wife- swapping, he hasn't been very interested.

I do think that Her Majesty quite fancies me and that, if she weren't married and head of a sovereign nation, I could be just the bit of rough she's looking for! Hellfire, I get a throbbing blue veiner just thinking about it!

You may come to one's garden party, Chubbs, provided you don't show your arse or have sexual intercourse with a pile of caviar like you did last time!

I always ensure that Her Majesty and Phil get the best seats at my shows. One day, I hope they'll return the favour and let me use the Royal Box...

ROY CHUBBY BROWN, CRACK INVESTIGATOR in The Case of the Maltese Hard-On – Part One

Another open and shut case for Middlesbrough's most famous dick.

Chicago is a big city where action is only two blocks away from danger and excitement is downtown from death.

Unfortunately this is Middlesbrough and it was as quiet as a sparrow's fart.

My name is Brown, Chubby Brown and although people think I'm a fanny magnet I'm actually a crack detective.

It was 11.00am on a Monday morning and I'd already finished a case. It was a case of Newcastle Brown Ale and my head was buzzing like a nun's dormitory after lights out.

There was a loud knock on my door.

"It's open" I growled.

A tall, blonde woman walked through the door. I could see she was going to be difficult – everyone else opened it first.

She had an hourglass figure – except that most of the sand was up top. She must have had a 42 inch chest. Suddenly I found myself saying something stupid.

"It's a bust!"

"Pardon?" she enquired.

I apologised for an old joke but then something clicked (I made a note to see my osteopath). "Don't I know you. Aren't you that hooker who operated behind the gasworks? Sophie...Sylvia...Sandra...Sarah... I know the name..."

"It's Sadie"

Of course! You were on the tip of my tongue."

"Quite probably", she replied.

"I remember when you were caught by the fuzz."

"Yes. And being swung by the tits wasn't much fun either!"

Sadie sat herself down on my desk then got up again. Then sat down again. Then got up again. That decorative paperweight shaped like a dildo was proving to be a real attraction.

"Are you a dick?", she purred.

"Well, people have called me that – and also 'fat bastard' and 'git face'", I answered. She leant forward so I could see right down her blouse; she was the sort of girl who'd come joint first in a Zeppelin race.

"No, I meant, are you a dick – a detective?", she continued.

"Yeah", I retorted. "Can't you see that sign on the door - *Chubby Brown P.I.* It stands for Private Investigator".

"Oh. I thought it stood for 'Pissed Idiot'". She pouted and continued, "Is that a pistol in your pocket or are you just pleased to see me?"

I pouted back, "It's a pistol. If I was pleased to see you it would look like a 155mm howitzer – or at least a rifle."

I carried my trusty 45 all the time. "Chubby, your gun's like you", Sadie purred.

"Do you mean that it's primed and ready for action?", I enquired.

"No", she sneered, "It's half cocked with a hair trigger."

"My ex-wife didn't complain."

"No, but I heard she left because you were firing blanks."

Sadie sure knew how to hurt a guy (they probably paid her extra for it).

Suddenly she was down on her knees in front of me. I thought she was suggesting this instead of a retainer but she shattered my delusions...

"Chubby" she pleaded "You've got to help me out!"

"Certainly" I replied, taking her arm and leading her to the door.

She shook herself free. "No Chubby. You don't understand. I want you to find something for me."

"Listen lady, I know you've lost your virginity but there's nothing I can do about that!"

"It's not that. It's my brother. He was due to spend a few days with me last week but he never showed up. I think he's been kidnapped!"

"Do you have a lead?" I enquired.

"Yes. But that's for my kinky clients who pay extra. Leave my professional life out of this", she glared.

"No. I meant why would anyone want to kidnap him?"

"He's a police informant with a lot of enemies."

I feared the worst. Another local grass had died just two weeks ago. This was the gay informant 'Lefty Lionel'. He'd been found in a motel room covered in blood – some bum had split on him. There could be a connection.

"I'll take the case", I announced. "A hundred a day plus expenses."

"Great!" she said.

"But you'll have to go to bed with me."

"What's that got to do with it?"

"Well, I'll be working under cover..."

TO BE CONTINUED...

CELEBRITY BOLLOCKS

A GREAT SCRATCH 'N' SNIFF COMPETITION FOR ALL THE FAMILY!
THE SMELLS ARE CLUES TO WHOSE BOLLOCKS ARE WHOSE!

HOW TO PLAY

1. Get a coin and rub over each pair of bollocks in turn.
Don't use your fingers. They'll smell of bollocks forever after.

2. Stick your nose up against the bollocks and inhale.

3. Identify the famous celebrity by the smell of their bollocks.
(If you don't have a good sense of smell, or don't want to sniff a
celebrity's bollocks, cryptic clues are provided under the pictures).

4. Write down the answers on the coupon. For example, if you think
the owner of pair of bollocks B is Bobby Davro, write his name in the
space. (You'd be bastard wrong, but you could do it).

5. Stick this book out in the garden because otherwise it'll reek
your house out.

GREAT
PRIZES
TO BE
WON!

A . CLUE; He was a 'SPLASH!' with Darryl
Hannah and had the Gump-tion to be in
Philadelphia for an award.

B . CLUE; He's got a bastard fifteen inch dick,
tells great jokes and has probably shagged your
missus.

C. CLUE; He's humped the Queen.

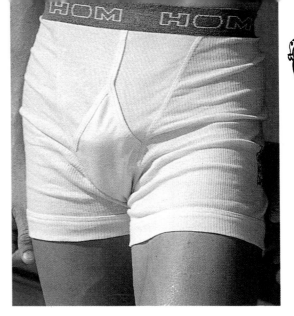

D. CLUE; Won Wimbledon Ladies Singles three years running.

ENTRY FORM

I have correctly identified the owners of the 'Celebrity Bollocks'

A...

B...

C...

D...

NAME...

ADDRESS...

....

Tiebreaker:
"I would like to catch a whiff of Trevor MacDonald's bollocks because
[Please answer with your reason in less than 12 words]

BOTTOM COMPETITION

Last month's competition was won by Mr J Major of 10 Downing Street, London, who correctly identified the smell of the EU Commissioner's bottom. Congratulations, Mr Major. Consolation prizes are on their way to virtually every other sodding politician in the country.

MY APPEARANCE ON MASTERMIND

I might not be a brainbox but compared with my missus, I'm a bloody genius. She really is a stupid twat. I caught her in bed with the milkman and she shouted to him, "Quick! Pretend you don't know me!"   She could never, ever, hope to appear on Mastermind - but I did, once.

Magnus: May we have our next contestant please.
[CHUBBY TAKES THE CHAIR]

Magnus: Your name?
Chubby: Roy 'Chubby' Brown.

Magnus: And your occupation?
Chubby: Filthy bastard.

Magnus: And your specialist subject?
Chubby: Shouting 'Piss Off!' after everything you ask.

Magnus: Good luck Mr Brown. You have two minutes on your
         specialist subject starting now.

Magnus: Who was the second man to climb Mount Everest?
Chubby: Piss off!

Magnus: Correct. Who wrote the American National Anthem?
Chubby: Piss off!

Magnus: Correct. What god did the Incas worship?
Chubby: Piss off!

Magnus: Which Pope said...
Chubby: Piss off!

Magnus: Correct. Well interrupted. How deep is a fathom?
Chubby: Piss off!

Magnus: Who succeeded Edward II to the English throne?
Chubby: Piss off!

Magnus: Correct. Name the two sons of Hercules
Chubby: Piss...

Magnus: I'll need a little more than that...
Chubby: Off!

Piss off · · ·

08

Magnus: Correct. Which Russian political leader was exiled to Siberia in 1923?

Chubby: Pass

Magnus: Where would you expect to see the Southern Cross?

Chubby: Piss off!

Magnus: Correct. What is the earth's rarest element?

Chubby: Sod Off!

Magnus: Incorrect. You should have said 'Piss off!'. Which vessel currently holds the world record for the quickest crossing of the Atlantic?

Chubby: Piss off!

Magnus: Correct. What did Einstein say...

[THE BLEEPER GOES OFF]

Magnus: I've started so I'll finish. What did Einstein say about mass and light?

Chubby: Piss off!

Magnus: Correct. Mr Brown, at the end of that round you have scored ten points. You passed on just one. The political leader exiled to Siberia in 1923 was of course, Piss off!

WHY MIDDLESBROUGH TOWN COUNCIL GET ON MY TITS

Did you know that there's only one place in the whole bastard world that has banned me from performing? It's not Vatican City. It's not Jerusalem. It's not even Tehran. It's Middlesbrough – my home bastard town.

There was a time when I *could* play Middlesbrough. That's before a new council took over. I should've known I was in sodding trouble when they first asked me to change my own bastard name.

MIDDLESBROUGH
DISTRICT AND PARISH COUNCIL

ENTERTAINMENT AND LICENCING POLICY GROUP
(PUBLIC MORALS WORKING PARTY)

Dear Mr Brown,

As you know, this Parish council prides itself on being non-sexist, non-racist and non-sizist. Therefore, in order to avoid offending those members of the community who are considered to be of above average weight, you must change your middle name from Roy 'Chubby' Brown to one that is more politically correct.

Any of the following would be acceptable to us: Roy 'Circumferentially Advantaged' Brown / Roy 'Generously Proportioned' Brown / Roy 'Person of Size' Brown / Roy 'Ample' Brown / Roy 'Big Boned' Brown / Roy 'Burly' Brown / Roy 'Strapping' Brown.

You will no doubt be glad to hear that we will allow you to retain your surname since we do not feel that it is sufficiently offensive to those non-white members of the community.

Yours faithfully,

Mike Hunt

As if that wasn't enough cheek, they then tried telling me what I could and couldn't say.

MIDDLESBROUGH
DISTRICT AND PARISH COUNCIL

ENTERTAINMENT AND LICENCING POLICY GROUP
(PUBLIC MORALS WORKING PARTY)

Dear Mr Brown,
We have noticed that a large part of your act concerns
jokes made at the expense of your wife, pertaining to her
genitalia and specifically how this part of her anatomy,
in your opinion, has the odour of various aquatic species.
If you insist on making jokes about fish, may we suggest
the following (these were contributed by the executive
council committee and while we are not professional script
writers, we do feel rather pleased with our efforts:)

Acceptable jokes about fish

Q: What did the boy fish say to the girl fish?
A: Your plaice or mine?

Q: What travels along at the bottom of the sea
   wearing a crash helmet?
A: A motor pike and side carp

Q: What goes dot dot dot, dash dash dash under the sea?
A: Morse cod

Q: Why are fish clever?
A: Because they always travel around in schools

Yours faithfully,

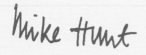

Well. I wasn't using any of these shite jokes so then they tried to rewrite the rest of my act for me. This is what they sent me.

MIDDLESBROUGH
DISTRICT AND PARISH COUNCIL

ENTERTAINMENT AND LICENCING POLICY GROUP
(PUBLIC MORALS WORKING PARTY)

Dear Mr Brown,

We notice from your recent performance at the Civic Hall that you have not taken on board our recent comments.
In order to demonstrate what is and what is not acceptable to this council we have had no option but to *insist* upon the following changes to your routine:

Unnacceptable routine
It was my turn to go into the doctors. I took my trousers off and asked him to have a look at my dick. It was all shrivelled, like a Walnut Whip. He took one look and told me that after I go for a piss I should shake it-not wring it out! Then I told him that every time I sneeze I get a hard-on. He asked me if I was taking anything for it and I said, "Yes. Pepper!

Acceptable routine
It was my turn to go into the doctors. I said, "Doctor, I think I'm a pair of wigwams". He said I must be too tense. Then I told him I thought I was a thief and he asked if I was taking anything for it.

Please find enclosed with this letter suggested changes for the rest of your act. We have no alternative but to ban you from performing in this town and its environs if these changes are not carried out forthwith.

Yours faithfully,

Mike Hunt.

Well, I just carried on my act as usual but this time I introduced a whole load of new gags about the useless bunch of tossers that masquerade as councillors. Needless to say the whole lot of them had no sodding sense of humour.

MIDDLESBROUGH
DISTRICT AND PARISH COUNCIL

ENTERTAINMENT AND LICENCING POLICY GROUP
(PUBLIC MORALS WORKING PARTY)

Dear Mr Brown,

Following an emergency meeting of the Parish Council last night there was an overwhelming vote in favour of banning you from performing in Middlesbrough. Forever. I should also like to refute in print the following allegations made during your act:

a)   That the Chairman of the Entertainments Policy Group (Public Morals) was doing it doggie fashion and broke his leg when he fell off the kennel

b)   That the Chief Executive of the Entertainments Policy Group (Public Morals) was going to stop being a flasher - but decided to stick it out for another year

c)   That the Secretary of the Entertainments Policy Group (Public Morals) suffers from epilepsy - but it's great when she's giving you a wank.

Yours disgustedly,

Mike Hunt.

There was only one response left..

In the interests of free speech sign this form, cut it out and send it to the address shown.
If you don't want to damage your book, go and buy another copy, you tight-fisted 12lb bag of shite.

WE DEMAND JUSTICE!

FREEDOM FOR THE MIDDLESBROUGH ONE!

To: **ENTERTAINMENT AND LICENCING POLICY GROUP
(PUBLIC MORALS WORKING PARTY)**
MIDDLESBROUGH TOWN AND COUNTY COUNCIL
PO BOX 99A,
MUNICIPAL BUILDINGS
MIDDLESBROUGH

We, the undersigned think it's a disgrace that Roy 'Chubby' Brown, one of Middlesbrough's most famous residents and composer of 'Do The Backscuttle' should be banned from performing in his own home town.

It's like Jesus not being allowed to speak in Bethlehem, Michelangelo not being allowed to paint in Rome or Cilla Black not being allowed to sing in Liverpool!

You should be concerned with the things that are relevant to councils like wasting residents' money on beanos to your twin town, messing up the one-way system and giving lucrative contracts to all your mates – not whether comedians are 'acceptable' or not.

So how about it, Middlesbrough Council? Don't be a bunch of gits! Let Chubby perform!

Signed ....

Date..

14 USES OF A USED TAMPON

- Bait when you go shark fishing

- A convenient, tasty snack for vampires

- Cocktail decorations in a hard-core lesbian bar

- Emergency bung for a nose bleed

- Cheap but colourful Xmas decorations for your tree

- New form of conkers for an all-girls school

- Designer earrings for your wife

- Touch-up brush for lipstick

- Emergency red felt pen

- Pretend mouse to keep the cat amused

- Hang them in the wardrobe so all your clothes smell of stale twat (look, I didn't say they were sensible uses, did I?)

- Hang them from a wide-brimmed hat to keep the flies away (well maybe that's a bad idea...)

- Stick them in pets' ears on bonfire night to stop them being frightened

- Making a decorative paint finish for your walls – well, you've heard of 'rag rolling' haven't you?

WIN TWO FRONT ROW TICKETS TO SEE MY SHOW!

All you have to do to see my great live act is to tell me how to get into Sharon Stone's knickers.

Send your answers c/o the publisher's address at the front of this book.

GO ON - GIVE IT A TRY.
SOMEONE HAS TO WIN (I HOPE)

ON THE ROAD

I've got a Ford Clitoris. I call it that because every twat's got one. (I also call it that because when I leave it in a car park I can never find it). I couldn't afford the version with an airbag so mine's got a blow- up doll instead. In an accident she inflates. It might not protect me, but it's sure to take my mind off my injuries until the ambulance arrives. But the best way to avoid accidents is to pay attention to road signs at all times - making sure you know what they *really* mean..

Condom machine nearby

Tit wank ahead

No limp dicks

**Warning.
My missus approaching**

**Impotence doctor
ahead**

**Impotence
specialist ahead**

I've got the horn

**I haven't got
the horn**

**Humps for
1/2 mile**

Jammy bastard!

**Danger!
My wife opening
her legs**

Blue Video

Mother-in-Law

UNZIPPED

Pissed motorist

Very Pissed Motorist

A screw
(well, seen from the top)

**My wife's got a
headache**
(again)

Ringpiece

Shite car

Huge dick with one bollock

CHUBBY'S GUIDE TO MEETING A GIRL'S PARENTS

Meeting your bird's parents for the first time can make you nervous. When her father shakes your hand you're thinking "I hope he can't tell this was down his daughter's knickers 20 seconds ago!" The important thing is to be honest; it pays off in the end...

PART 1 – PERSONAL DETAILS:

FATHER: I hear you met Deidre in your local pub.
CHUBBY: That's right. I took one look at her bristols and thought, "Whorrr! I'll 'ave some of that!"

FATHER: What do you do for a living?
CHUBBY: Swear and make jokes about my bird's minge.

FATHER: Deidre said you live nearby.
CHUBBY: It depends if I'm shaggin' at my other bird's place or not.

FATHER: Did you have a nice evening out?
CHUBBY: Yeah! You haven't lived until you've had it off in the back of a taxi!

PART 2 – SMALL TALK:

FATHER: We think Deidre takes after her mother.
CHUBBY: Why? Does she go like a train as well?

FATHER: Nice weather we're having.
CHUBBY: Yeah. I like it when it's sunny; all the birds come out in their short dresses and you can see enough to qualify as a gynaecologist.

FATHER: Have you seen any good films lately?
CHUBBY: Nudge, nudge. You want 'em, I can get 'em. A pony a tape – or a monkey if there's a pony on the tape, if you catch my drift, eh, eh?

FATHER: Would you care for a drink?
CHUBBY: Yeah. I've got this pube stuck in my teeth and I just can't get rid of it

PART 3 – TRYING TO ESTABLISH WHETHER YOUR INTENTIONS ARE HONOURABLE

FATHER: Do you know Deidre well?
CHUBBY: Well, I've shagged her, if that's what you mean.

FATHER: Do you see yourself as a family man?
CHUBBY: I've already got three kids. They live with their mothers.

FATHER: Could you provide for Deidre?
CHUBBY: If you're talking about my manhood there's more than enough to go round.
Just ask your wife.

FATHER: Do you believe in the sanctity of marriage?
CHUBBY: I reckon that your Deidre could suck a golf ball through a hosepipe!

FATHER: Welcome to the family, son. I'm glad you're not a lying bastard like her last boyfriend!

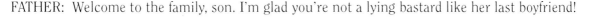

POP STORY

When I started out in showbiz I used to be a Donna Summer. That's Pop Rhyming Slang for 'drummer'. Donna Summer – Drummer. Get it, you dozy twats?

Why did we talk in Pop Rhyming Slang? Was it so we could talk in secret? Was it a condition of the Musician's Union? Was it because we were mental? No. It was just because we were a bunch of Stevie Nicks. You know, full of Barry White.

Anyway, this is something that happened to me...

It was after a gig and I was sitting in this **Jean Michel Jarre,** drinking a few cold **Billy Jo Spears** when this **Lionel Bart** comes up to me. She looked like she was on the **Kids From Fame** and asked if want to go back to her **Ace of Bass** for some **T-Rex.** I thought what the **Jeff Beck!**

When we got there I was dying for an **Eartha Kitt** so I rushed into the **Frank Zappa.** By the time I'd finished the lights were off and she was naked in **Right Said Fred.** I noticed she was a bit **Mariah Carey** and her chest was a bit **Take That** but I didn't give a **Diana Ross.** I was ready for a **Billy Bragg** or even some **Charlie Mingus** but first she insisted on giving me **Simply Red.**

After a few minutes I was **Jimmy Cliff.** She took me in her **Beautiful South** and I **Georgie Fame.** My **Thelonius Monk** was dripping all down her **Jeff Lynne.**

Afterwards I needed to go back to the **Barry Blue** for a **Brenda Lee** so I got up and put the light on. I couldn't believe my **Humble Pies.** Between her legs, instead of a **Johnny Cash** she had a **New Kids On The Block!** Instead of a **Mel & Kim** she had a big **Carlos Santana!**

'She' was a **Paul Weller** in drag! A fucking **Steely Dan!**

"Oy!" I said. "Get away from me, you bloody **Perry Como!** You're **Brian May**, you are, and you're not putting your **Grace Slick** up my **Gary Glitter!**"

"Oooh! Don't get **Lionel Richie!**" the **Chris Rea** said. He thought I was **Jackie Trent.**

I felt **Dave Hill.** What had happened was **Belinda Carlisle.** I put my clothes on and ran out.

The next day I told my **Tom Waites** what happened. They pissed themselves laughing and called me a right **Paul Anka!**

CHUBBY BROWN INVITES YOU TO TAKE...THE DUZ DOORSTEP CHALLENGE!

WHY THE DISCOVERY OF FIRE WAS SO IMPORTANT

It was probably just like that, you know. Well *someone* had to be the first one to light their own farts, didn't they? For most men, lighting their own farts is an everyday event – like brushing their teeth – or having one off the wrist. But me, well, I like to consider myself a bit better than that. I see myself as something of a connoisseur of lighting one's own farts. An artist with the anus; a wizard with the wind; a specialist of the sphincter; a virtuoso of the rectum (alright, I know there's no bloody alliteration. I'm not Roy 'Chubby' Wordsworth am I!) There's more to lighting your own farts than you might think. It's not just holding a lighter to your arsehole and letting one rip. It's all down to technique – control over your ring-piece is important, as is split-second timing and the address of your nearest 24 hour accident and emergency ward. If only people took a little more trouble when lighting their own farts, the results would be far more rewarding...

Putting the art back into fart

With a little patience and a lot of chicken vindaloos you too could be lighting your own farts with style and panache.

Some classic Fart Flames:

- **Vesuvius**
- **Flamed Grilled Whopper**
- **Solar Flare**
- **Bunsen Burner**
- **Petrol Tanker Carnage**
- **Nagasaki**
- **The Hindenburg**
- **George And The Dragon**
- **Towering Inferno**
- **Blow Torch**
- **Arson Attack**
- **F-15 Tomcat afterburner**
- **Crepe Suzette**
- **Colon Conflagration**
- **Real Log Fire**
- **The Other Blackpool Illuminations**
- **Olympic Torch**

ROY CHUBBY BROWN, CRACK INVESTIGATOR in
The Case of the Maltese Hard-On – Part Two

It was shaping up to be a lousy day.

Sadie's brother had disappeared like a cucumber in Holloway Jail and I had nothing to go on – the office toilet had been blocked up solid since Wednesday.

Furthermore, the bits of the jigsaw puzzle just wouldn't fall into place. I'd finished the fluffy black kitten but the cute little tabby's face remained incomplete and I cursed my auntie for buying it for me last Christmas.

At least I was on a hundred a day retainer, which started the moment I put aside my jigsaw and took the voluptuous Sadie over my office desk.

4 1/2 pence worth later, we lay together on the floor of my office, our breath coming in short pants (how we'd both got our heads stuck in my Y-Fronts I just couldn't figure).

"I've never had sex like that before!' she gasped.

"You mean sex that good?"

"No, I mean sex with one elbow in my mouth and another in my kidneys".

I decided it was time to get serious about the case, before Sadie could point out any of my other short-comings. 'What did your brother do for a living?' I asked.

"He was a proctologist," she replied. "Does that disgust you?"

"No, I admire a man who's prepared to start at the bottom,'

"About a month ago, he rang to say he'd got his hands on something very interesting,..."

"What, like a multi-coloured colon or something?" I replied, confused.

"No, he said he'd got the hard-on,"

"Is that something he usually tells you? And doesn't it bother his patients?"

"Chubby, have you ever heard of the Maltese Hard-On?"

I recoiled in shock. The Maltese Hard-on! The legendary fabulous jewel encrusted dildo of the Crusaders! Three feet long and two feet thick, and inlaid with precious rubies, emeralds and sapphires, it had mysteriously appeared and disappeared throughout its bloody history. 'Sister, the Maltese Hard-On is bad news," I told her. "Any man who owns it tends to die horribly. I guess it's their own stupid fault for trying to stick something that big up..."

"My brother found it!" Sadie interjected. "Where. he didn't say..."

"I can guess..."

"One last clue. He told me he was going to celebrate this Hard-On by going out to the swankiest gay clubs in Middlesbrough and 'getting his rocks off.' "

"He believed in mixing business with pleasure then," I observed. 'So, Where do you go in this town to get your rocks off?"

"The sex change clinic?" Sadie smirked..

"Was that a wise-crack?" I asked

"No," she replied, hoisting up her skirt. "This is a wise-crack. It knows algebra and geometry, and can name all the American presidents".

"I definitely prefer a wise-crack to a smart-arse," I retorted. "Lady, I don't know the gay scene in this town. Not at all. Not one bit. Not even slightly. I know nothing. Zip. Zilch. Zero. I'll have to call my snatches for information..."

"Don't you mean snitches?" she asked

"No, I call them snatches 'cos they're always fannying around and never there when you want one."

Twenty minutes later however, I had the information I needed and we were speeding in my car towards Middlesbrough's seedy North Orsmby district and the docks.

Our first port of call was The Club-a-Go-Go. Too late. It was gone.

We had better luck at the Pink Coconut Bar and Contemporary Arts and Crafts Centre. As we pulled up to the kerb I recognised a councillor from Middlesbrough District and Parish Council standing outside. The leather biker's cap, chains and cycle shorts were no disguise from a trained eye. He was carrying something very large and very phallic wrapped in a blanket.

"That's Councillor Felching," I told Sadie. "He's on the Entertainments Committee. He hands out all the club licences."

As we watched, someone came out of the door. It was disgusting, unnecessary and several passers-by narrowly missed being splashed. It was Joey 'The Hamster' Griddlesthwaite, one of the biggest crooks in town. He ran all the gay rackets - the amateur dramatics, street performers, contemporary dance - even the really sleazy, grubby things like mime acts and face-painting. He gave Felching a briefcase, took the object in the blanket and the two men went inside.

"There's something very dirty going on here..." I muttered.

"You think he might be bent?"

"Lady, that's a foregone conclusion. I mean he's taking bribes too – and that might have been your brother's Hard-On he was holding.'

There was only one way to find out what was going on inside. I'd have to go in. But the dress code was distinctly raunchy. I did the best I could. I threw off my PI's mac, dropped my trousers and pants around my ankles and waddled across the road to the club entrance, yelling, "hey, I'm ready!"

I wasn't fooling anyone. I was swiftly thrown out by the bouncers, which hurt more than anything I'd ever experienced in my entire life.

"I'm not licked yet," I gasped, tears streaming down my cheeks as Sadie rushed to comfort me. "Cover my back!" I snarled, "I'm going in..."

TO BE CONTINUED...

CHUBBY'S SITCOM STORY

One day, I escaped from my *Nearest and Dearest* and went out with my *Friends, Shelley, Frasier, Terry and Julian* for a drink at the *George And The Dragon*, I said, *'For The Love of Ada*, who's that? She has an *Absolutely Fabulous Bottom'* I was *Bewitched!*

'That's *Roseanne* Muir, *Terry and June's* lodger. She lives next door to *The Simpsons'*, replied *Frasier*. 'Her husband recently gave up *The Ghost and Mrs Muir* has been horny ever since. You couldn't count *The Lovers* she's had *After Henry* passed on – *Mr. Bean, Father Ted, The Fenn Street Gang, The Brady Bunch, The Partridge Family, Jeeves & Wooster* and a veritable *Dad's Army* of older *Men Behaving Badly*, as well as *The Management* of this pub and even the occasional *Red Dwarf*.

Believe me, *Three Up Two Down And Mother Makes Five* is nothing unusual for her! *Get Smart!* Forget her. *No, Honestly,* take my advice. *Love Thy Neighbour?* – she never stops. Her legs? *Never The Twain* shall meet, mate!'

'Are You Being Served?' asked the barmaid.

I ordered two glasses of *The Last of The Summer Wine*, gave her some *Brass* and went over to *Roseanne*, although we were *Perfect Strangers*. *'Allo, Allo'*, I said, offering her a drink.

'Cheers!' she replied.

Now *Roseanne* was a bit old. She had definitely *Gone To Seed* and looked like she had *One Foot In The Grave*. I thought, *Oh Brother!'*, because I usually prefer *The Young Ones*, and wouldn't normally sink *Solo*, but she was *Young At Heart* and they say *Life Begins At 40*. I could tell that we were *Birds of a Feather* and soon we were *As Thick As Thieves*. She told me she needed a *Man About The House* and maybe even *The Odd Couple*. She was obviously gagging for it and cried, *'Home James!'*.

Soon, we were in a *Taxi* and *Going Straight* back to her place. Within a *Hancock's Half Hour,* we were in bed together. (I love *Girls On Top!*)

'Do you sleep with everyone you meet?', I asked.

'Only Fools and Horses' she replied.

Previously, she had gone out with both *Steptoe and Son.*(Keep it in *The Family* was her motto.) But they were *All Gas and Gaiters*, completely unable to *Get Some In.*

'Fawlty Towers?' I suggested.

'Yus My Dear' she replied. 'What's your excuse? Do you have trouble getting it to *Full Stretch, Time After Time?'*

'Never Mind The Quality, Feel The Width,' I smiled.

'Bilko!' she snorted

'Mind Your Language!' I replied.

It was *A Fine Romance.* We had *Happy Days* throughout *Spring and Autumn. From May to September, The Two of Us* did it everywhere, even *On The Buses* and with *My Wife Next Door* with our *2.4 Children* – but definitely *Not In Front of The Children* if they were *Watching.*

Once we went out into the country and did it in *Fresh Fields*, disturbing a *Robin's Nest* and upsetting *The Squirrels, Nightingales* and *Butterflies.*

But our relationship was going in *Ever Decreasing Circles.* We were overdoing it and one day she was ill. She was in *Agony*. I checked her temperature. *It Ain't Half Hot, Mum.*

'Is there a *Doctor In The House*?' I shouted. 'My girlfriend has *Rising Damp!*'
The Doctor arrived. *'Please Sir!* Can you save her?' I pleaded 'We're both *Men Of The World.* Be straight with me. Can you give us a *Second Chance?*
'Her *Health and Efficiency* are both fine,' he replied, applying some *Surgical Spirits.*
'She's just having too much sex. At her age, she really shouldn't be *Open All Hours.* My advice is *Don't Drink The Water* and try *Different Strokes.* Eat *Honey For Tea* with some *Bread,* cut out the *Porridge* and *Mash* and you'll soon be enjoying *The Good Life* again.
'We followed his advice and lived *Happy Ever After.*

NOW THAT'S WHAT I CALL CHUBBY'S RECORD COLLECTION!

CONDOM CLASSICS!

Accidents Will Happen – Elvis Costello

Baby I'm Scared Of You – Womack and Womack

Get It On – T Rex

Accident Waiting To Happen – Billy Bragg

Cover Me – Bruce Springsteen

Rubber Bullets – 10cc

Stop That Girl – Chris Andrews

The Safety Dance – Men Without Hats

Johnny Remember Me – Johnny Leyton

Baby What A Big Surprise – Chicago

No Other Baby – Bobby Helms

20 CATCHY VD HITS!

Great Balls of Fire – Jerry Lee Lewis

Love Is Contagious – Taja Sevelle

Love Strain – Kym Mazelle

Bad Love – Eric Clapton

The Clapping Song – Shirley Ellis

Shake The Disease – Depeche Mode

Burning Love – Elvis Presley

Fireball – Deep Purple

Contagious – The Whispers

Doctor Doctor – Thompson Twins

Dangerous Sex – Tack Head

Fever – Madonna

Fire Down Below – Shirley Bassey

Thunderball – Tom Jones

Green Onions – Booker T and the MGs

Tainted Love – Soft Cell

Everything's Gone Green – New Order

Infected – The The

My Love Is Dangerous – Freddie Mercury

The Danger of a Stranger – Stella Parton

Solid Gold Sex Aids!

Are Friends Electric? – Gary Numan
Buzz Buzz A Diddle It – Matchbox
All By Myself – Eric Carmen
Like Clockwork – Boomtown Rats
Good Vibrations – Beach Boys
Wind It Up – Prodigy
Heavy Vibes – Montana Sextet
Automatic Lover – Dee D Jackson
Machinery – Sheena Easton
Electric Lady – Geordie
Vibeology – Paula Abdul
Candle In The Wind – Elton John
Sisters Are Doin' It For Themselves –
  Eurythmics and Aretha Franklin
Love Machine – Miracles
Gonna Get Along Without You Now – Trini Lopez
Alone Again, Naturally – Gilbert O'Sullivan
Only The Lonely – Roy Orbison
Gold Finger – Shirley Bassey
Sex Machine – James Brown

PULSATING PREMATURE EJACULATION SMASHES!

Half A Minute – Matt Bianco   It Only Takes A Minute – Take That
Don't Make Me Wait Too Long – Roberta Flack   Can't Keep It In – Cat Stevens
Something Got Me Started – Simply Red   Come Together – Beatles
10 Second Bionic Man – Kinky Machine   Suddenly – Billy Ocean
I Can't Wait – Stevie Nicks   There Goes My Everything – Elvis Presley
Gone Too Soon – Michael Jackson   Glad It's All Over – Captain Sensible
Feels Like The First Time – Foreigner   Zoom – Fat Larry's Band
Don't Leave Me This Way – Communards   Greased Lightning – John Travolta
Flash – Queen   Get A Grip On Yourself – Stranglers   Shoot Shoot – UFO
I'm So Excited – Pointer Sisters   Ain't No Stoppin' Us Now – McFadden and Whitehead
Don't Throw Your Love Away – Searchers   What A Waste – Ian Dury and the Blockheads
Splish Splash – Bobby Darin   Ready Or Not, Here I Come – Delfonics
Excitable – Amazulu   Jumping Jack Flash – Rolling Stones   It's All Over – Cliff Richard
Easy Come, Easy Go – Sutherland Brothers   I Can't Help Myself – Four Tops
Sat In Your lap – Kate Bush

FARTING GOLD

Blowing In The Wind – Peter, Paul & Mary

In The Air Tonight – Phil Collins

Two Pints Of Lager And A Packet Of Crisps Please – Splodgenessabounds

Beautiful Noise – Neil Diamond

The Wind Cries Mary – Jimi Hendrix Experience

The Sound Of Silence – Simon & Garfunkle

The Air That I Breathe – Hollies   Wind Beneath My Wings – Bette Midler

Wayward Wind – Jimmy Young   Wind Power – Thomas Dolby

Rocket Man – Elton John   Let It All Blow – Dazz Band

Cut The Cake – Average White Band   Strange Brew – Cream

Blow Away – George Harrison   Backfired – Deborah Harry

Something In The Air – Thunderclap Newman

Wild Is The Wind – David Bowie   Bourne On The Wind – Roy Orbison

Purple Haze – Jimi Hendrix   We Gotta Get Out Of This Place – Animals

Four Strong Winds – Neil Young   Four From Toyah – Toyah

Four More From Toyah – Toyah

PROSTITUTE POP HITS!

Goodnight Girl – Wet Wet Wet
The Name Of The Game – Abba
Brass In Pocket – Pretenders
Back On The Streets – Saxon
Caught By The Fuzz – Supergrass
Streetlife – Crusaders
Can't Buy Me Love – Beatles
It's A Game – Bay City Rollers
Good Girls Don't – The Knack
Heaven Is In The Back Seat Of My Cadillac – Hot Chocolate
Another Piece Of Meat – The Scorpions
Pleasure Boys – Visage
One Night In Bangkok – Murray Head
Price Of Love – Every Brothers
Back Street Love – Curved Air
Money Honey – Bay City Rollers
Down On The Corner – Creedance Clearwater Revival
Put Your Money Where Your Mouth Is – Rose Royce
I'm Every Woman – Chaka Khan
Boom Boom – John Lee Hooker

BIG NOB Chartbusters!

8 Miles High – The Byrds
Deep Wide And Tall – Aztec Camera
Too Big – Suzi Quatro
How Long? – Ace
Eight By Ten – Ken Dodd
The Big Hurt – Maureen Evans
Hanging Around With The Big Boys – Bloomsbury Set
Big In Japan – Alphaville
Can You Handle It – DNA
Hurt So Good – Susan Cadogan
Jumbo – Bee Gees
Big 10 – Judge Dread
If It Don't Fit Don't Force It – Kelly Patterson
How Deep Is Your Love? – Bee Gees
In Too Deep – Genesis
My Jamaican Guy – Grace Jones
I Love You Because – Jim Reeves

Celebrity Interview – ROY 'CHUBBY' BOND

INTERVIEWER: Roy, it's not often that we get the chance to talk to a secret agent, a real life 007...

CHUBBY: I'm not an 007, just 003$^1/_2$. That means I haven't got a licence to kill - just permission to kick someone in the balls and run off.

INTERVIEWER: I see. But I understand that a film's been made about one of your missions.

CHUBBY: That's right - 'Octopussy' - it's about a woman with eight fannies.

INTERVIEWER: And in it you drive an amazing car...

CHUBBY: It's an Aston Martin DB5 - the 'DB' stands for the 'Dogs Bollocks'. It's great - the passenger seat flies into the air; the number plate swivels round; smoke pours out of the back and oil gushes all over the road... Just like my old Skoda.

INTERVIEWER: Does it handle well?

CHUBBY: Bloody marvellous. When I drive down cobbled streets I arrive shaken but not stirred.

INTERVIEWER: Tell me about your early days working for British Intelligence.

CHUBBY: 'British Intelligence'? That's a laugh. It's like saying 'Italian Courage' or 'French Hygiene'...

INTERVIEWER: I see...but do you remember your first day at the Secret Service?

CHUBBY: I couldn't forget it - it was so secret they didn't tell me the address and it took me three days to find the bastard office.

INTERVIEWER: You were working for 'M'?

CHUBBY: That's right. But I upset him by calling him by his real name, 'Marlene'.

INTERVIEWER: Did he give you your first case?

CHUBBY: No. That was 'Q'. It was a Black Samsonite with a concealed camera.

INTERVIEWER: Did that come in useful?

CHUBBY: Not really. I couldn't find it.

INTERVIEWER: Did you undergo lots of training?

CHUBBY: Yes - including how to kill a man with just one finger. Mind you, what threat can a man with one finger pose?

INTERVIEWER: You've said on previous occasions that you felt that 'M' didn't like you. What gave you that impression?

CHUBBY: Well, all agents are issued with a cyanide pill for use in emergencies - he told me it was a bastard Tic Tac. And we're all given code names. Other agents were called 'Hammer', 'Leopard' or 'Steel' - I was known around the office at 'Fat Git'. They also said I was a double agent.

INTERVIEWER: A double agent?

CHUBBY: They were teasing me about my size.

INTERVIEWER: I see.

CHUBBY: And you know that after a mission, most agents are picked up by a Navy submarine well I was given a rubber ring and a picture of Dover.

INTERVIEWER: But that didn't stop you going on some really dangerous missions?

CHUBBY: No. My first operation involved a cunning villain who combined the deadly evil of Blofelt and Odd Job - he was called 'Blo-Job'.

INTERVIEWER: Where were you at the time?

CHUBBY: I was concealed in Sharon Stone's bedroom.

INTERVIEWER: And that was all according to plan?

CHUBBY: Not really. I should've been watching the docks in Budapest.

INTERVIEWER: But Chubby, all secret agents like you have got a reputation for being suave and sexy.

CHUBBY: I know. I had a torrid affair with my trusty secretary, Miss Moneybox.

INTERVIEWER: You mean 'Miss Moneypenny'?

CHUBBY: No. Miss Moneybox. I always left a deposit in her slot.

INTERVIEWER: But I bet you had to seduce lots of foreign female agents.

CHUBBY: Well the first time I did this was in Moscow. I was naked and she said 'Is that why they call you $003^1/_2$'.

INTERVIEWER: What did you say to that?

CHUBBY: I just said I was the spy that came in from the cold.

INTERVIEWER: And that was the mission where you were captured?

CHUBBY: Yes. It was at this point I realised my true worth. Instead of exchanging me for one of their spies, the Russians wanted to trade me for six tins of Spam and a pair of jeans

INTERVIEWER: Is that all?

CHUBBY: Well not exactly. They later dropped the demand for the jeans and five of the tins.

INTERVIEWER: When you were captured were you interrogated?

CHUBBY: Yes. But I cracked when they hit me in the bollocks with a sledgehammer.

INTERVIEWER: But I thought all agents are taught how to stand up to torture?

CHUBBY: Well I must have missed that particular lecture.

INTERVIEWER: But after all your adventures do you still like working for the Secret Service?

CHUBBY: It's better than being The Man From Uncle. They're constantly fighting their deadly enemy, T.H.R.U.S.H. I have enough trouble with crabs.

INTERVIEWER: But you must get asked, 'Chubby, what's the best thing about being a secret agent?'

CHUBBY: That's easy. Pussy Galore...

MY HOME TOWN

TEESSIDE WANTS TOURISTS!!!

Promote tourism to Teesside and win a Fish Supper for Two!

What makes Middlesbrough marvellous, Redcar remarkable and Stockton striking?

We want YOU to help us promote tourism to Teesside and get it known as the pearl in the North East's oyster – rather than "some bloody place up North between Leeds and Sunderland".

All you have to do is devise a campaign to attract visitors to the area. It could be an advertisement, a poster, a jingle, a poem – whatever you like – providing it promotes Teesside in all its splendour!

Issued by the 'Tourism In Teesside Society' (T.I.T.S.)

Well, I've always fancied myself as a bit of a poet (you might have read my limericks "There was a young girl in a punt", "There once was a spaceman on Venus" and "This pretty girl from Dunnilingus"). Anyway, grabbing my ball point, this is what I sent in...

My Home Town – By Roy Chubby Brown (see, the bastard rhymes already!)

There's many exotic cities
Like New York, Paris and Rome
But the best spot on earth
Is the town of my birth
It's the place I call my home

It's on a famous river
Not the Nile and not the Seine
It's the River Tees
Which down wind in a breeze
Can smell just like a drain

It's Middlesbrough of course
Up on the North East coast
It might be boring
And get you snoring
But to me it's got the most

St Mark's Square, the Pyramids
They're all quite uninspiring
The Taj Mahal
Is frigging dull
The Empire State's quite tiring

The leaning tower of Pisa
And China's old great wall
Monuments in these cities
Just get on my titties
'Cos Middlesbrough's got it all

You can keep your Sydney Harbour Bridge
You can stuff your Central Park
I'd rather be
With a lass on my knee
At the gasworks after dark

And what about our landfill site
Or the old abandoned mine
The sewage farm
Has lots of charm
And the foundry is just fine

It might not be tropical
It might not have the sun
This is a town
Where it pisses down
But it still won't spoil your fun

Now Bondi Beach might have the surf
And Acapulco has the heat
But for oil and turds
And dead sea birds
Our sea front can't be beat

We may not have any posh hotels
Like a five star Ritz or Hilton
But a B & B
That's known to me
Once booked in Peter Shilton

We don't have Gucci or Versace
Or any of those posh nob shops
We've got the best
And you'll be impressed
Our 'Mister Bi-Rite' is the tops

We used to have an opera house
Where the finest singers played
But where it stood
Is something good –
A huge amusement arcade

We don't have mime or ballet
We don't put on King Lear
If you're one of the farts
Into performing arts
There's the panto every year

Our lasses don't have lovely tans
The sun is not that bright
There's soot in their hair
From the dirty air
And they look a sickly white

Now you might think I'm a stupid twat
To stay here all the year
To live in a dump
That smells like my rump
But I really am sincere

I love this town; it's wonderful
Now you might laugh and scoff
But I hope you see
It's home to me
So you can all F. Off

Tourism In Teesside Society (T.I.T.S.)

Dear Mr Roy Chubby Brown,

We've read right through your poem
But try as hard as we might
We can't help but come to the view
That it's a pile of shite.

Yours sincerely,

V. Jynu.

BUM RAP

By Chubby B.

You can call me Chubby - Chubby B
And I'm your randy, rappin' MC

I love to rap when I get the time
I'm a wiz with words and ready with rhyme

I take the stage and I jump and prance
You can hear me break wind as I break-dance

This here is a song dedicated by me
To my favourite part of anatomy

I'm talking about the dear old 'rump'
It's great for sitting on – or taking a dump

It's got many names and here are some:
There's 'Buttocks', 'khyber' and the 'bum'

Some other words, kinder to the ear,
Are 'backside', 'behind' or the 'rear'

People who think that they're superior
Insist on calling it their 'posterior'

Overseas they might use a different name
But the part they're describing is still the same

In all the places where Americans strut
They call it a 'keister' or even a 'butt'

Not a nation to beat about the bush
They also use 'ass', 'buns', 'fanny' or 'tush'

Over in France they think it's debonair
To refer to the rear as the 'derriere'

But me, well look, a man of my class
Is just content to call it an 'arse'

You can tell that I'm a bottom man
Who studies them whenever he can

I'm a buttock worshipper
A real hindquarters connoisseur

It's quite amazing how they all vary
Some are smooth and some are hairy

Some are rough and some have dimples
Some are covered in horrible pimples

Some are blotchy and others scabby
Some are soft and very flabby

Some just wobble like a jelly
Some are perfumed –
some are smelly

But the nicest type of any botty
Is one that's firm and not at all spotty

Now I've reached the end of my song
I'm sorry it's gone on a bit too long

I hope you don't think my latest rap
Is like its subject...full of crap!

(I like this title. It's got a certain ring to it...)

UNZIPPED

SHOULD YOU DUMP YOUR MISSUS?

Is your missus crap? Should you ditch her?
Take this handy five minute test and find out!

TAKE A CLOSE LOOK AT HER. WHAT'S THE FIRST THING YOU NOTICE?
A   A strong feeling of nausea (-2)
B   She's a fat cow (-3)
C   The tattoo (-4)
D   Breakfast on her flannelette dress? (-3)
E   A flawless complexion (+3)
F   Giant knockers (+7)
G   Scabs that are positively medieval (-4)
H   The same knickers on that she was wearing last week (-3)
I   She hasn't shaved again (-2)
J   The uncanny resemblance to Kim Basinger (+15)
K   The uncanny resemblance to Will Carling (-8)

WHAT'S THE FIRST THING SHE SAYS TO YOU WHEN SHE SEES YOU?
A   Mine's a pint of furniture polish (-2)
B   How about a threesome with my blonde and nubile best friend? (+4)
C   How's this for a fart! (-1)
D   It's not what it looks like! The milkman accidentally lost his contact lens in my minge and he's trying to find it (-3)
E   Hello darling. Let's go to bed (+11)

HOW WOULD YOU BEST DESCRIBE HER FIGURE?
A   Nonexistent (-3)
B   Sexy (+3)
C   Frigging' fat (-2)
D   Sleek and Parisienne (+5)
E   Whey-hey! (+5)
F   Horrible (-3)
G   From the back, she looks just like Robbie Coltrane (-5)
H   From the front, she looks just like Robbie Coltrane (-6)
I   Out of control (-2)

HER PERFUME CAN BEST BE DESCRIBED AS
A   Totally overwhelmed by other bodily odours (-3)
B   Sophisticated (+4)
C   Worse than the cat's bum (-2)
D   Like someone's weed on a burning rubber tyre [-5]
E   Harry Ramsden's No5 [-10]

WHAT IS SHE PARTICULARLY GOOD AT?

A Stuffing down entire family sized anchovy and pineapple pizzas in under a minute(-4)
B Oral sex (+12)
C Doing silent but deadlies under the bedsheets (-3)
D Turning a blind eye to the tarts you keep picking up (+4)
E Making Dawn French look like Suzanne Charlton (-2)
F Picking up builders (-2)
G Crotch scratching (-2)
H Giving you the clap (-6)
I Picking and flicking when she thinks you aren't looking (-2)
J Spending all your friggin' hard earned wages (-13)

WHAT IS YOUR MISSUS MOST AFRAID OF?

A Not pleasing you in bed (+2)
B You finding out about her and the rugby team (-2)
C Her pet rat escaping (-4)
D Not having your dinner on the table in time (+13)
E Soap and water (-2)
F Losing your love and respect (+2)
G A blowback when she lights her farts at parties (-3)
H You finding out that your best mate gave her scabies (-5)
I Not being able to blow all your wages at the Bingo in a single evening   [-5]

SHOULD YOU DUMP YOUR MISSUS NOW?

SCORE: Less Than Zero – YES.

MORE THAN ZERO – No.

HISTORY OF THE BACKSCUTTLE

When you're doing the Backscuttle do you ever stop to think who invented it? Or are you too busy holding on for dear life?

It actually originated many thousands of years ago and has inspired many great men and women ever since. As an expert in the field (I'm a B.Sc – a Bachelor of Scuttleology) I'd like to share its history with you...

25,000 BC
The first recorded Backscuttle took place between early man and a Tyrannosaurus Rex. Steven Spielberg is planning a major film to capture this historic moment –"Jurassic Poke".

1000 BC
Apart from owning a Technicolour Dream Coat, Joseph was also famous in the Old Testament for his enthusiasm for the Backscuttle. Appalled by his son's behaviour, Joseph's father banished him to Egypt and he was forced to leave his brothers behind.

55 BC
Julius Caesar introduced the Backscuttle to Britain and remarked, "I saw, I conquered – I came".

1492
Christopher Columbus introduced the Backscuttle to the New World when he caught a stowaway on board his ship and made him work his passage.

1609
While doing the Backscuttle, explorer Henry Hudson accidentally came upon the Northwest Passage – one of his most famous discoveries.

1540
Backscuttling King Henry VIII destroys the monasteries after they refused to let him enter the priesthood.

1590
William Shakespeare was a great fan of 'Ye Olde Backscuttle'; it inspired him to write 'A Midsummer's Night Dream' and create the character of Bottom. He was especially pleased with this character's name because it had a ring to it. (The Backscuttle also inspired Shakespeare to write 'Two Gentlemen of Verona' and 'As You Like It').

1645
During the English Civil War Oliver Cromwell used strategies based on the Backscuttle. At the Battle of Naseby his army came up the rear and surprised Charles I, who had not expected an assault on his flanks by a determined roundhead.

1802
Horatio Nelson (not to be confused with Fellatio Nelson) often indulged in the Backscuttle with his shipmate, Hardy. He was later promoted to Rear Admiral.

1839
An important event in the history of the Backscuttle – the final thrust of the Anglo–Afghan war took place this year at the Khyber Pass.

1841

Backscuttle afficianado, P T Barnum opens the world's first three–ring circus.
(Him and two other arseholes)

1848

Lawman Wyatt Earpe was killed after infamous desperado 'Backscuttle Bill' came into town and shot up the sheriff.

1857

The British brought the Backscuttle with them to India and many people were forced to endure the Black Hole of Calcutta. This inspired the famous book, 'A Passage To India'.

1876

Celebrated German composer Richard Wagner set the Backscuttle to music, stunning Europe with the breadth and magnitude of his Ring. Critics attacked it for its bum notes.

1896

First modern Backscuttle Olympics held in Athens. There were over 120 entrants.

1922

At the height of the Great Depression, Backscuttling was the most popular past-time in America as virtually everyone was hard-up (and the rest had their backs to the wall).

1927

During Prohibition Backscuttle gangs ruled Chicago. You couldn't walk the streets without being involved in a stick-up.

1939

Neville Chamberlain bent over backwards to please Herr Hitler.

1940

In between dog-fights, Battle of Britain pilots indulged in inter–squadron Backscuttling. They soon earned the nickname 'The Brylcream Boys' (well, Vaseline was on ration).

1956

Taken by surprise and given the Backscuttling of his life in a Soho alleyway, celebrated playwright John Osborne was furious and inspired to write 'Look Back In Anger'.

1969

Neil Armstrong and Edwin Aldrin carried out the first Backscuttle on the moon. Armstrong commented that it was "One small step for a man; one giant aaahhhhh...aaahhhhh...ohhhhhhh"

1992

Roy Chubby Brown jumped on stage during the Eurovision Song Contest and performed 'Do The Backscuttle'. He was later disqualified for this illegal entry.

1995

After three years of Backscuttling in an Indiana jail, 'Iron Mike' Tyson made a spectacular comeback in the ring. His opponent was a very sore loser.

THE ROMANTIC CHUBBY

"I wouldn't give you my last Rolo if you were in a diabetic coma!"

PLAYROY

ENTERTAINMENT FOR LONELY HOUSEWIVES   DECEMBER 1995 VOL II No. 4

UNZIPPED

THE HELMET. THE HEARTACHE. CHUBBY REVEALS ALL!

CRABS!
And other seafood recipes.

TITS OUT!
Keeping birds away from your plants.

BEAVER!
Dam building with these furry friends.

DOGGIE STYLE!
And other pet's clothing.

STIFF!
Is there a cure for rheumatism?

83

THE GREATEST SHOW OFF-EARTH!
MY FORTHCOMING TOUR OF THE UNIVERSE!

When this season's over, I'm going to boldly go where no man has gone before - and put on a show! Yes, I'm going to blast off and go on tour amongst the stars, taking my act to a whole new audience! All the expenses for my epic year long tour of the universe are being paid for by Middlesbrough District and Parish Council - which is strange, because I thought they didn't like me. Recently, I gave a press interview setting out my plans...

INTERVIEWER; So, you're going to be the first blue comedian in space?
CHUBBY; That's right, aye.
INTERVIEWER; How do you feel?
CHUBBY; Well, I sort of get my hands and..touch things. Strange bloody question that is!
INTERVIEWER; No, I mean...oh, never mind. Where will your epic voyage begin?
CHUBBY; Middlesbrough Space Centre
INTERVIEWER; They've got a space centre in Middlesbrough?
CHUBBY; Well, when I say space centre. It's a bit of waste ground out by the new by-pass, but it'll be OK, as long as no-one's playing footie there when we want to use it. Otherwise we'll have to wait
INTERVIEWER; Are you using an American rocket?
CHUBBY; No, the lads at Middlesbrough Tech have knocked something together for me. It's much cheaper and quicker apparently. You don't need a countdown to take off. You just light the blue touchpaper and retire.
INTERVIEWER; It sounds a bit dodgy.
CHUBBY; The most difficult thing has been finding a two hundred foot tall milk bottle.
INTERVIEWER; Well, once you've taken off, do you actually know how to steer the rocket?
CHUBBY; No, I don't know the first thing about navigating in space. They asked me where you'd find Saturn's Ring. I said,'On Uranus.' Then they said, 'where's Pluto?' I had to guess; 'At Disneyland with Mickey and Goofy?'
INTERVIEWER; If I were you I'd be worried.CHUBBY; What, about getting lost in space?
INTERVIEWER; No, I'd be worried about being a fat northern bastard.
CHUBBY; Oy, oy! I do the funnies, OK?
INTERVIEWER; Certainly. I just couldn't resist it.
CHUBBY; Well, that's fair; Your missus couldn't resist me...
INTERVIEWER; Ahem...Mr Brown, are you at all worried about shooting off into space?
CHUBBY; No, I've been practising at home. It's very useful. It helps me prepare for splash-down as well!
INTERVIEWER; No. I mean, there you are on the launch pad ready to go. Aren't you worried about blasting off?
CHUBBY; Look mate, if you had a 4,000 ton rocket under you, I think you'd be farting yourself stupid too!
INTERVIEWER; What about while you're in-flight? Are you concerned about asteroids?
CHUBBY; No. I've packed some Preparation H.
INTERVIEWER; What do you think about shooting stars?

84

CHUBBY; I think it's quite wrong. John Lennon was a lovely guy.

INTERVIEWER; Isn't there anything at all that really scares you about your daring spaceflight?

CHUBBY; Well, I'm a bit wary of these 'Black Holes'. Apparently they suck everything they come across. A bit like my missus. It's the gravity, y'see. At their heart they're super dense. Again, just like my missus.

INTERVIEWER; And where's your first show?

CHUBBY; I'm playing the Alpha Centauri Roxy on October 1st.

INTERVIEWER; Do you think these strange, completely alien life forms will get your jokes?

CHUBBY; They should do. I've always gone down well in Wales...

INTERVIEWER; Supposing you arrive on the planet and there's no intelligent life...

CHUBBY; That's never stopped me in Dudley...

INTERVIEWER; Supposing they're hideous, mutated, strange creatures with a completely different mentality to us on Alpha Centauri...

CHUBBY; No chance of that. All my in-laws live in Sunderland.

INTERVIEWER; Their air may not be breathable. How will you communicate with them?

CHUBBY; I'll just talk through my helmet, like I usually do.

INTERVIEWER; What about when the tour's over and you head home? Are you worried about achieving re-entry?

CHUBBY; I've never had any problems with that. Ask your missus.

INTERVIEWER; Finally, have you any advice for people who are interested in the stars?

CHUBBY; Yes. Never, ever look at The Sun through a telescope. Page 3 isn't any clearer, and you could go blind.

INTERVIEWER; Good luck, Chubby!

CHUBBY SAYS,
"SAY IT WITH FLOWERS"
"Piss off!"

CHUBBY AT HOME

My missus knitting me a willie warmer...

ROY CHUBBY BROWN, CRACK INVESTIGATOR
in the Case of the Maltese Hard-On - Part Three

There were only two things that prevented me from getting into the Pink Coconut Club - and they were six and a half feet tall and beefier than ten Big Macs. What's more they also had chips on their shoulders.

Like making love to a fat bird, I knew I was on to something big but could see that finding a way in would be difficult. But I was determined to get inside the Club and see just what - or who - was going down.

I approached the main door with a flan. Then I realised that in my haste I'd misread my Detectives Handbook and what I should have done was prepare a plan. There was only one thing for it – I'd have to think on my feet. Mind you, it was difficult enough walking on them with the new shoes I was breaking in.

I decided to ad lib and as I approached the bouncers I said the first thing that came into my head, "I'd love to cover Anthea Turner in marmalade and pick out all the bits of orange rind with my teeth". They gave me a blank look so I said the second thing that came in my head.

"Excuse me", I said politely, "I want to go in your entrance".

"That's what they all say", they pouted back. "Anyway, this is a strictly all-male club. To get in we need proof of sex".

I dropped my trousers and showed them. They said they needed more proof. I was insulted and anyway, it was cold.

I fumbled for an excuse, dropped it, picked it up again and in desperation said, 'Look. I'm a friend of Julian'.

That seemed to do the trick. They asked me if I was carrying a concealed weapon but I said it was just the way my trousers hung. Then the bouncers said they'd have to check and they frisked me. Seventeen times. Once they were satisfied (I think it was on the fourteenth or fifteenth time) they waved me in.

Inside the club I soon found myself in a long, dark passage.

Eurrrgghhhh! So that's what it felt like! I withdrew, knowing that this sort of move might give me away, and mingled with the other club members. I hoped no one would blow my cover – or anything else.

Keeping my head down, I managed to blend in well with the crowd and kept my eyes open for a clue that Sadie's brother was being held against his will (or against anything or anyone else).

I walked into a large hall where a disco was in full swing. There was more leather here than a chapter of Hells Angels riding a heard of Fresians. Before I knew it, someone had tugged me on to the dance floor.

The caretaker cleaned up the mess with a bucket of sawdust and I found myself staring into the eyes of Councillor Felching. He asked if I was gay so I mimicked an old movie camera with my hands to go along with the charade.

He gave me a strange look – which wasn't surprising since he was the spitting image of Marty Feldman, then he took me in his arms. Fortunately our attempts on the dance floor ended in confusion when we both tried to lead and I was saved from an embarrassing tango - not to mention an even more embarrassing black bottom.

I made my apologies and then made my way out of the hall – watching my back along every step of the way. Suddenly the heavy bass beat of the music was punctuated by a piercing scream.

Unlike most of the club members, it was my heart that was in my mouth as I ran towards the sound. Soon I found myself in a corridor leading up to a small room near the fire escape.

The cry rang out again and my blood, like freshly-squeezed orange juice and ten day-old milk poured into the same glass, curdled. With total disregard for my safety I crept on all fours up to the room, not wishing to make a sound.

I pushed the door open slightly and I was immediately slapped in the face by the acrid smell of smoke and vaseline. What I saw in the dingy room was a picture of wickedness and depravity. Even the bulb hanging from the centre of the ceiling was bare.

Speadeagled on the table and trussed up like a chicken was Sadie's brother. Facing him, with his trousers round his ankles, was Joey 'The Hamster' Griddlesthwaite, the crooks' leader. At least, I assume Joey was their leader. From where I was standing he definitely looked like a Mr Big.

It was obvious that Sadie's brother had been subject to an unpleasant – not to say biologically unnatural – form of torture in an attempt to get him to squeal – and by the sounds I'd heard, it was working.

In Joey's hand was the Maltese Hard-On, glittering in all its priceless glory. It looked like Joey was about to use it on Sadie's brother. Gazing at its size, I knew it wouldn't be long before he cracked.

I had to act, and act fast!

"Now is the winter of our discontent!" I blurted out as I burst in.

In one move I took off one of my shoes and smashed the single light. In the confusion I untied Sadie's brother and grabbed the Hard-On. There was a yell. I let go, apologised to Joey and grabbed the real Hard-On.

I ran like I'd never run before – sideways, with a sort of hopping motion. Burdened by Sadie's brother and the Hard-On I was making slow progress.

"Hold it right there!" I spun round and saw Joey with a gun pointed at me. At least I think it was a gun - it was quite dark. Whatever it was, I didn't want it going off in my face.

I had to bluff my way out. "If you shoot I'll drop the Maltese Hard-On and it'll smash into a million pieces".

"You wouldn't dare!"

"Just try me!" I threatened.

Taking this as his invitation, Joey dropped his gun followed by his trousers and threw himself at me. One blow to the head with the Maltese Hard-On was enough to bring him to his knees – a position that came automatically to him.

Within ten minutes Sadie's brother was recovering in hospital with his Hard-On and the police chief was reading Joey his rights.

"For kidnapping and GBH you'll be going down for a long, long time".

"Aren't I the lucky one!", said Joey as he was lead away.

Another chapter in my life over, I wearily mounted the stairs to my office (it seemed sexually normal after all the comings and goings at the Pink Coconut Club). As I turned the corner something caught my eye. It was the bastard fire extinguisher on the wall and it friggin' hurt. Then I noticed a cardboard box outside my office door, tied up with yards and yards of string. In fact it was covered in so much string that the only word I could read on the box was 'Samsonite'.

Just my luck - another case that needed unravelling.

THE END

MY FAMILY TREE

CHUBBY UGG
Invented fire but immediately stamped it out because he thought it was dangerous. Also invented cave painting but received first clip round the ear for writing on the walls.

OLD TESTAMENT CHUBBY
Noah's next door neighbour. When the Flood came, instead of animals, Old Testament Chubby packed his ark with buxom blondes and crates of Light Ale. Never seen again.

KING CNUT
You may not believe this but I'm descended from royalty. This is my distant ancestor King Cnut. Apparently he was dyslexic.

CHUBBY DA VINCI
Claimed to have invented the world's first steam-powered penis enlarger. Ridiculed by his peers, who thought he was just pulling their plonkers.

PROFESSOR CHUBBY OF VERSAILLES
Marie Antoinette's GCSE English teacher. He took her for both the written and the oral, where he helped her to get her tongue around the hard parts and prepared her for intercourse. The trouble was, when he wanted to conjugate, she declined.

JOLLY JESTER BROWN
The earliest comedian in my family and Court Jester to Edward II. Famous for the joke, 'Why dost his majesty wear a crown? So he dost knoweth which end to wipe!' (Also famous for whimpering 'don't kill me!' all the way to the gallows.)

CHUBBY SHAKESPEARE
While his older brother concentrated on plays and Sonnets, my great great great great great grandfather Chubby Shakespeare specialised in Limericks. His major works, 'There was a young lass in a punt...' and 'A game young lad with a duck..' have long since been lost. Shame.

ROBINSON 'CHUBBY' CRUSOE
Accidentally marooned on a desert island with 15 serving wenches and a vat of whipped cream. Tried to signal passing ships by lighting a signal puddle and waving a small sock at them from as far away as he could get. When eventually rescued by a passing clipper, his first words were, 'Piss off, you bastards!'

OLD FARMER CHUBBY

An early pioneer of animal husbandry - for which he received a suspended sentence. Also famous for displaying his prize-winning cock at county fairs - for which he also received a suspended sentence.

MASTER BAFFLE 'EM BROWN

Slightly saucy comedian who combined cheeky patter with magic tricks. Not the best act to perform during the height of the witch hunts. Cruelly referred to at his time of execution as 'Britain's hottest comedian'.

BOOM-BOOM BROWN

Entertainments officer on the Titanic. The man who got the captain to agree to a game of 'Blind Man's Bluff'.

CHUBBY VON RICHTOFEN - THE RUDE BARON

World War One's most unsuccessful fighter pilot. His technique of swearing at enemy pilots, baring his bum and making frantic rude gestures proved no match for synchronised twin machine guns and he was shot down. A terrible crash-landing left him minus his joystick and most of his undercarriage. Never married. He left me his helmet in his will (I keep it in a pickle jar.)

CHUBBY THE KID

He could get his weapon out and shoot faster than any man alive (Now I know where I get it from...)

CHUBBY CHAPLIN

One of the great silent film comedians. His career ended abruptly when talking movies came along and people could hear what he was really saying.

CHUBBY CHUCKLES

Entertainment officer on the Hindenburg. (You'd think my family would have learned not to light their farts by now, wouldn't you..?)

CHUBBY EINSTEIN

A brilliant man who combined the laws of *Time* and *Relativity*. He discovered that Time is actually twice as long when you spend it with the wife's relatives. (For this he was made 'Professor of the Bloody Obvious' at Cambridge.)

TRAVEL TIPS No.1
How to Swear like a native – wherever you are.

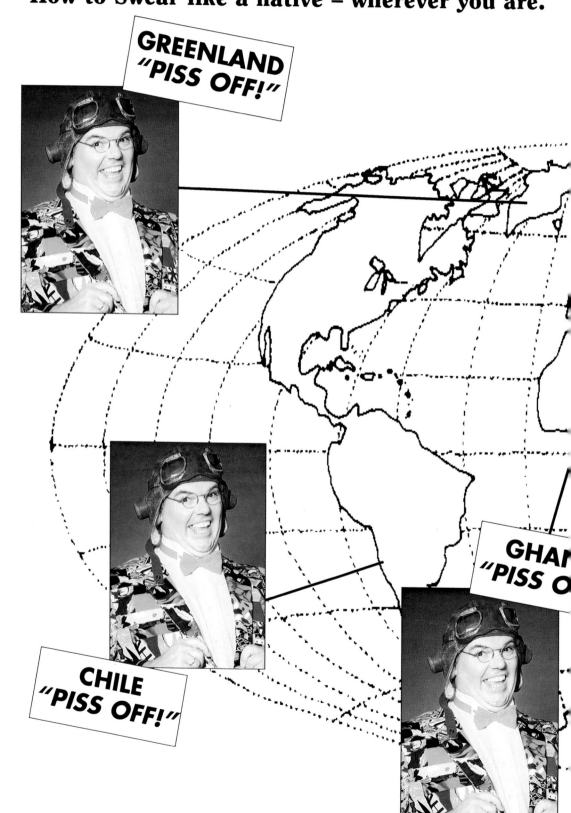

GREENLAND "PISS OFF!"

CHILE "PISS OFF!"

GHAN "PISS O

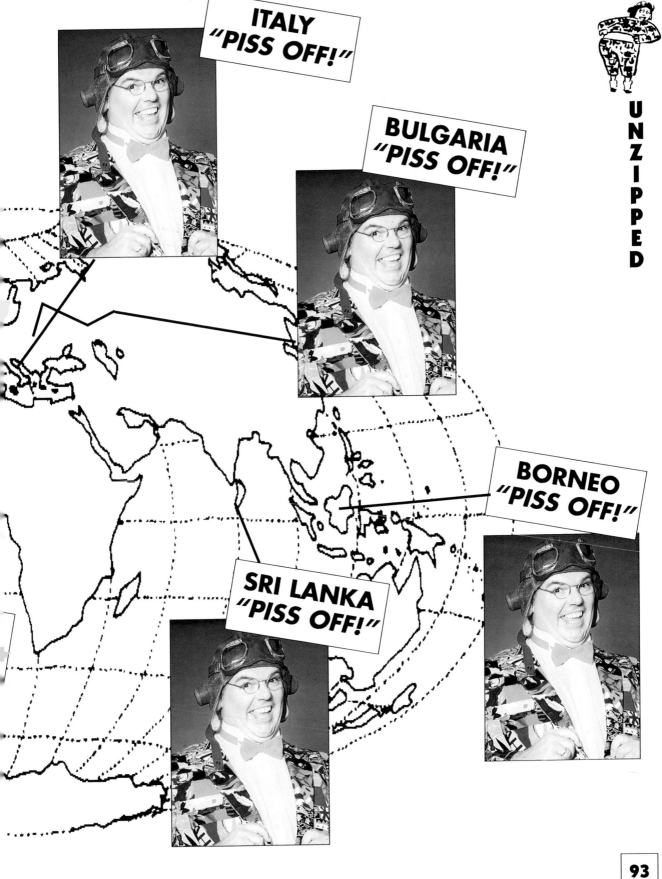

C
H
U
B
B
Y

B
R
O
W
N

ACKNOWLEDGEMENTS

The publishers would like to thank the following for their kind help and assistance:

The Stockholm Academy of Swearing

The Museum of Rude Words, Madrid

The Directorate of Bad Language, Minsk

The Library of Cussing, Nebraska

The Institute For The Advancement of Expletives, Vancouver

Musee de Filth, Paris

Oxford University (Dept. of Profanities)

The phrase 'bollock face' appears by kind permission of Hugh Grant

The word 'shite' appears by kind permission of Take That (UK) Limited

Roy 'Chubby' Brown appears courtesy of his wife (providing he's back by 7.30pm because she's going to bingo)

THANK YOU
FROM CHUBBY

A huge thank you to my manager George Forster for his overwhelming support and all his team who have helped in my success. But most of all, sincere thanks to my thousands of loyal fans up and down the country who give me the encouragement and confidence that all comedians need when they step into the spotlight.

FROM MARK LEIGH & MIKE LEPINE

When they saw the manuscript most of the people who've helped in this book shat themselves. To save them undue embarrassment, we'd like to thank Philippa H██████ L█████, Debbie L██████, Gill L█████, Adam L█████, Alison MacL██, Judy M██████, Richard P██████, Adrian S██████████ and Darren at Horatios.

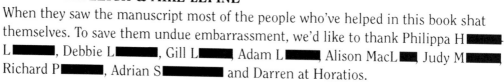

If you would like to receive a free Roy Chubby Brown
merchandise catalogue Telephone: 01661 820588
or write to, The Roy Chubby Brown Fan Club

    No. 3 Pont Park
    Berwick Hill
    Pontland
    Newcastle Upon Tyne NE20 0JX

THE END